Searching the Pearl

Searching the Pearl

The Poetry of Lyle Osland

ADALENE OSLAND

TORONTO, ONTARIO

Published in Toronto, ON, Canada by
Uncapped Publishing.

For information contact:
Uncapped Publishing TORONTO.CANADA
http://www.uncappedpublishing.com

ISBN: 978-1-7771062-6-3

First Edition: November 2023

DEDICATION

My husband Lyle's written thoughts have been published for our wonderful children: Michael, Paul, Lisa, Lara and their families. However, I am sure that they mean more to me than to anyone else. They reveal how much I meant to him.

I have many cards and letters, sent even before we were married, that give me comfort every time I read them.

Lyle became a significant part of my life when I was 14. In many ways I became the confident person I am today because of his continual support for anything I wanted to achieve in life.

I have many pictures of his interactions with his children and grandchildren.

Unfortunately, his passing too early has left a huge void in the lives of me and his family.

He loved us all deeply and if he could see us today, he would be the proudest husband, father grandfather and great grandfather.

Dear Father,

May the meditations of my heart,
the thoughts of my mind,
and the words of my mouth
be always acceptable
in thy sight,
O' my Lord.

April 14, 1980

CONTENTS

IN LOVE FOREVER

REMEMBERING

FRIENDSHIP

MY MIND

INTRODUCTION

On April 14, 1980, my husband Lyle turned 43 years of age, and I wondered what to buy him for a birthday gift. I came up with the idea of collecting all of his creative written work in one place, so I purchased a book where he could enter his poetry. He began by writing a prayer to God.

On June 3, 2003, after a three-year valiant battle with cancer, Lyle passed on. In the difficult task of sorting through all of his belongings, I discovered Lyle's poetry. I realized that numerous scraps and pages still existed that hadn't been transferred into his book, so I began to copy all of his work into his book myself.

I was grateful to have his thoughts in his own handwriting on the original sheets of paper; however, being his greatest fan, I wanted to share his writing, especially with his family.

On the 20th anniversary of his passing, I decided to compile his body of work into a published form. His beautiful family and future generations will have this gift of his treasured thoughts. They will know how much I loved and respected their father, my dear husband.

I look forward to the day when we will be together again!

Adalene Osland, 2023

ABOUT THE POET

When Lyle was only three months old, his father died tragically on a construction site. Without the encouragement of a father during his developmental years, Lyle achieved a successful career that spanned five decades until his untimely death on June 3, 2003.

After finishing high school, Lyle studied at Queen's University for five years in their co-op accounting course. During university, he apprenticed with a small family business of chartered accountants. In his fifth co-op year he was recruited by a large firm. In 1961, Lyle graduated with excellent marks as a chartered accountant.

Although he was an accountant and auditor by day, he was a deep and philosophical thinker. Throughout our married life he would read different philosophers, and he had a deep desire to experience life to the fullest.

Whenever Lyle wanted to express his thoughts, he wrote them down on whatever was available. It could be a paper napkin after a meal or a bag that held a purchased book.

I am thankful for my husband's written thoughts. They are a comfort to me and a legacy for his beloved family.

Our love is faith and hope,
and joy
that makes our life so real

August 12, 1961 - St. Mathias Anglican Church, Etobicoke

IN LOVE FOREVER

TO ADALENE, MY VALENTINE

Our life is full
  of wonderment
As we listen to the
  mystery of
  beauty around us.

Like the mallards winging
  their way across the
  open waters
Our tiring flight is one
  of beauty
But the surface of life's sea
Is wild with rage and
  there is no peace
But that within us.
The rest is nowhere
  to be found.

Then with faltering flight
    we finally see
The peace within us
    can become
The peace without.

And we shall hear the
    sound of real
And listen to the
    mystery of love.

To you and this cause
I commit my life.

Feb 14, 1970

VALENTINE

Our love begins a new life
    as each storm passes by,
And from each storm we accumulate
    a strength and depth,
To us unique.

In the eons of time the reality
    of now is love, and
Our stay together, with its
    illusion of brevity,
Is forever.

Future, past, and present, they
    all become mere words
In the timelessness of our minds,
    wherein we dwell

Two as one.

February 14, 1971

FREEDOM

Adalene,

Live for the quiet moments amid the
chaos,
If there sometimes seems no place or time
to free your mind to live,
the answer is in your self.

So on this day of your thirty-second birth
remember your self and think anew
your place on the earth
and let it be.

Then will our minds
be free and aware
of the love of our
being near.

I Love You Near Me

1973

A TIME OF LOVE

Here and now we stand.
The wind behind and life in hand.
Ne'er before was there such peace.
When did the clouds first break,
Who remembers the first blossom
Of life renewed?
It came without event
From what fertile field
Grew our love?
Or did our love permeate
the barren soil
and germinate
the seeds our souls
so carefully preserved?

And now behold
    the beauty of a flower,
So simple, so pure,
    the bud of first creation
And where, from here?
No time nor direction
Has relevance
    in our evolution.
The earth, the skies
    hold in our eyes,
        the eternity of love
            let go.
To you, my darling,
    my simple flower of life
I give you peace
    and a field to grow.

Feb 14 / 75

A DAY TO REFLECT

Every year I feel an enrichment
    of the beautiful peace
        we share,
Coming closer to being here now
Let my quiet love
    still the murmurs
        of your every care
I am with you
    especially to-day.

TO ADALENE

Touching, touching,
Soul to soul
Evermore nearing
The elusive goal

Draw near with faith
And love unbound
Touch my soul
With ne'er a sound

Now broken the circle
Of living enclosed
Its limited gainless
Restrictions imposed

The cosmos unfolds
To beholding eyes
A world of bliss
For you and I.

November 28, 1975

DELHI AIRPORT

My darling, I sped away
    Looking for the infinite
    Not knowing where to look,
        or why
But being here helped me see
    the now-obvious simplicity
I am here as I am there,
    with God everywhere
God and guru with us when apart,
closer still, together
Infinite beauty in 'lands'
    unknown
Sketch before us, waiting for
    our meditative search
All to be reached within.

Our path is meant to be one,
One, with each other.
Our souls are close,
    yours and mine
Little needs to be said,
    communicating as we do,
With our own special
    vibration.
The golden pot is there
    before us
We have but to
    help ourselves.

April 26/77

IN FLIGHT: DELHI TO LONDON

Need I speak to thee of our love?
To light a candle to show you the sun?
It is obviously what we make it,
We have made it so beautiful
And the beauty grows
As the souls draw near
So that in the end
We will be eternally together
In unending bliss,
    One with God.

For God is our common unity
In whom, we shall never part,
He is our goal, not a vague,
    intangible idea,
But a blissful realization
As real as our lying together,
What the future beholds!

April 27 / 77

TO ADALENE

A toast to a year
    of significant changes
Cross new frontiers
    the consciousness grows

Together we go
    forward to sow
The seeds of our love
    In a future
        gentle and warm

Happy Birthday
    Love,
        Lyle

June 5, 1977

MY DARLING WIFE

O' how the flowers
    express our love
Each petal unfolding
    in the pearly den
A new face of affection,
    wonderment, bliss
Endless colours and shades
    soft textures and hue
How gently the breeze
    stirs life anew
We'll dance in the sunshine
    and sing our praise
Of our God-blessed lives
    and flower-like view
For the flowers and our love
    are one with God
Let us fill every day
    with our love
        Namaste

Lyle

February 14, 1979

AWARENESS

A new page, a new thought, a new day,
    a new moment,
Does one leaf matter from another?
Be where you are.
    And let it happen.

In a few minutes we will be together
    and yet,
I am with you now more than I will
    be then.
Our bodies are an illusion, as is time.
Whatever we have been, whatever we will
be,
    we are now.
    And now will never end.

The other pole of now is sleep
Whether for a night or forever
Sleep is nowhere never
Now is everywhere ever.

AUGUST 12, 1979

Eighteen years ago
by God's altar
we opened a new path,
not knowing tomorrow.

How we have brought
the joy surrounding us,
God only knows.

Like a soft guitar
we played cards
of peace and love.

And the promise of tomorrow
holds such beauty.

The vision grows clearer,
the lines run deeper
the goal draws nearer.

Whisper our love
o' my darling,
Gently feel his presence.

United, God cannot resist
the beckoning call
of our souls.

In love forever,
Lyle

GOD DREW A HEART

Adalene,
God must have known
our love
when he created Valentines
He must have
seen us touch
when He drew a heart
Praise God
for the promise
of our perfect love.

Happy Valentine,
Lyle

Yesterday is but a memory,
tomorrow still a promise …
but today is ours
to hold and live.

Feb 14, 1980

MY DARLING ADALENE

The day is just begun.
Our lives begin to open.
Feel the lifting of our wings
as we feel the joy
of flight, and the freedom
of God's presence

All my love,
Lyle

Nov 20, 1981

OUR LOVE

Our love fills every breath of air
  we breathe
Like ocean waves against the shore
  Our love wears down the rocks
    of worldly trials
    set in our path before.

Our love, my darling, is the
  essence of life,
The presence of Christ in us we feel,
Our love is faith and hope,
  and joy
that makes our life so real

I love you,
Lyle

Feb 3, 1982

MY DARLING ADALENE

This time spent will pass and we will be the better for it.

Close your eyes and I am beside you. Feel me with your mind. I can be one foot from you or thousands of miles and I am still as close.

Feel my love and I will feel yours. Think of our times together without talking. Those times are no different. We are together now.

I love you dearly,
Lyle

Oct 2 / 87

EMOTIONS

Beautiful it goes, on and on,
the music has stirred my depths.
And emotion turns me to the one I love.
I am, thou art, we are – beautiful.

I want to serenade you in the moonlight
and ride with you over the moors
and face the ocean winds together.

Every crescendo is the climax of a new
experience
Every note a stroke of our love.

Words are simply words but see how they
bind us
Listen to the tears.
They say so much.

You find me wandering, seeking, listening,
    unsatisfied, restless, then ecstatic, then
content.
One comes not without the other.
    In the quiet our hearts are in our eyes
    And beauty is again all around.
But the wandering stirs my depths and
that is where we really find each other.

ADALENE

My darling,
I tried to write you a poem
I tried to think of what to say
But nought would come
Only an image
of you and I
in love
You and I
alive
You and I
a universe,
Words
lacking everything
I want to say
My aspirations
locked in your heart
Hold me
Forever.

Lyle

Jan 21, 1988

REFLECTIONS

Here I am in the midst of life
with a moment to reflect on the past
a time to pay tribute to those you know
For the love that was there to last

We ask and we take but we think very
little
of all the demands that we make.
and few of the promises happily we give
were ever fulfilled for your sake

This life goes on a few things come clearer
Though why it is hard to say
Somehow the excitement of yesterday's
care
Seems a natural event for to-day

The gentle concerns we now take heed of
Somehow fit in an overall plan
I feel a need to tell you my love
and fill your heart full of my wine
So open your arms and take me enclosed
Let your love be replenished with mine.

OUR RENEWAL - GOD'S CALLING

To Adalene, my love,
Come home my little one
    Come home to me.
Forget your past
Your hurts and sorrows,
Accept the only love
    You know will last.

Don't struggle my daughter,
    Just let me in,
Let me bring light to your life,
    Know the joy I promise
Hear my word
    Feel the edge of the knife

Your sins I know so well
  Now you know my love,
Now you feel my pain
  How can it be so good
You ask?
  This surely can't be sane.

But even now you see only in part,
  A poor reflection as in a mirror
Yet to receive your crown.
  Come home my little one
Let me turn your world
  Upside down.

All my love,
Lyle

August 20/89

HERE WE GO

If we're gonna make it,
We gotta make it together,
Hand in hand, side by side.

The hearts 'n flowers of yesteryear
Are nice, as nice is nice
But to the sound of real they've died.

The age of freaks and rock is on us
We're getting with it an' we're gonna go,
Hang on baby for a beautiful ride!

The old success is too heavy
The old sex too tacky.
My, how the leaves have dried.

A new way, new hope, new friends,
Our drummer has changed his beat.
Our minds are no longer tied.

We're gonna make it baby,
And when we stand on the hill
Our hearts will open wide.

ALIVE

How alive I am!
I'm coming home!
I would not be with you as much as now
    if we were together.

The secret is to find the mystery but
    not to solve it
To live alive and show it.

The beauty in your eyes is unmatched
    in nature's mirror
It reflects the beauty of your love
    as well as your anger
And they are both still beauty, opposite
    poles of a common source

I love your love, I love your anger
I could not separate the two any more
    than I could
    The music from the notes or a poem
        from its words.

MY DARLING ADALENE

Today was a day without you,
no touch of your hand
no soft caress
no sparkling eye
no whispering voice
no prayer together,
a cold day of winter
alone in the Philippines

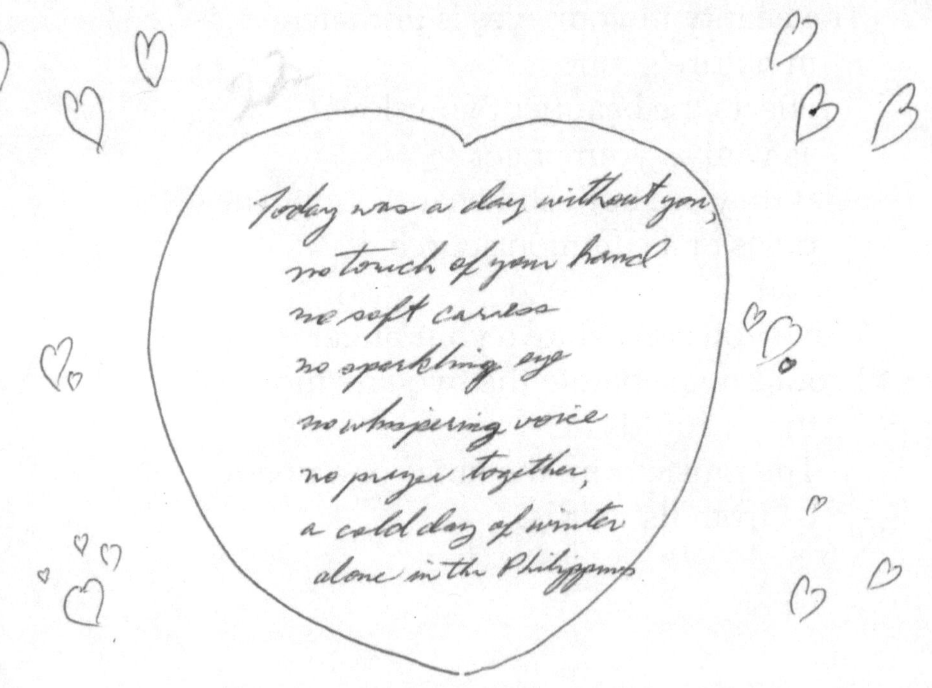

MY DARLING ADALENE

We have a dream you and I
where life is simple
and all we do is done
together.
Though great challenges come,
great victories still,
for you and I, in our dream
are closely held
in the bosom of our Lord.

We call on him
and he answers us
We give him our lives,
he enraptures our souls
and then will be our love complete.

We have this dream you and I,
That God truly is fulfilling
my dearest one,
I love you, I adore you, I praise God for
you.

Love forever,
Lyle

March 2, 1991

We feel a kind of spirit with you
of something being
when we're all here.

Photo taken in our West Vancouver Home, 1971.
Left to right: Michael, Lisa holding Lara, and Paul.

REMEMBERING

DINNER WITH PAUL
AT CHARLIE BROWN'S

"Mr. McCleary … my son Paul."
"Mr. Moll … my son Paul."
A table of honour
    saturated with service.
Bread
    … salad
        … more bread
            … cole slaw
More bread
    … steak
        … ice cream
How much can one boy eat?
what fun!
    a sip of wine … a puff of cigar
        such beautifully silly chatter
And laughs, … so many laughs
with a minor course of serious suggestions
    between steak and ice cream
        all well digested
A gentle piano
    and glistening eyes
        and talk of home.

A stroll after dinner
… study the fountain colours
… watch the funny people
and home.

What is the cost
of a boy's love,
give him your gladness
give him your sadness
give him your heart
of all,
give him his self
on an evening
such as this.

Sept 18, 1973

REMEMBERING

Once a year we may
Set aside a special day
To remember then, the one
Whose womb we swelled
Whose hand we held
To us, our radiant sun.

Throughout the year we had
Unquestioned love when sad
We took for granted all
You had to give
Without a thought
You seemed so strong and
tall.

Reflecting back we see
A solitary me
Looking for identity
And all the while
With just your smile
We gained serenity.
So know that now to-day
No less in any way
The centre of our being
Will hold your love
As the heart of the dove
Of peace.

Love, Lyle & Adalene

Mothers' Day, 1974

TO DON AND PAT, JUNE 21ST, 1975

A time for wishing, happiness,
a time for joining hands.
The fire warms our hearts
and none could part our ways.
Keep this moment,
don't let it pass.
and if in some small way
our love
can add to your joy,
be with this moment
and know we are one,
together.
May the beautiful future
always be here now.

Love,
Lyle and Adalene,
Michael, Paul, Lisa and Lara

TO GARY AND CAROL

A time to remember
your start together and where you've come,
we're happy to be a part.

We feel a kind of spirit
with you
of something being
when we're all here.

There is a beauty
that comes from two pairs.

Where'er you go
may you find the peace
of that spirit
you now have.

July 9, 1975

ALLAN AND IRENE TUMBER
2 TORRIDON LANE,
GLENROTHES, FIFE, SCOTLAND

From strange lands you came
  together,
With warmth and kindness
  for each other
Demanding not, wanting not,
Only giving your love.
And so you have come this day
  to express a beauty uncompared,
  proceeding directly from God
As brother and sister
  to man and wife
We offer you both
  our unconditional love.

Best wishes
God be with you.

Lyle and Adalene

June 22, 1976

MEMORY BURSTS

A boat trip, a waterfall,
Sunday at the farm
A game of crib, a look of love
These have kept me from harm

Memory bursts as a flower unfolds
Releasing its fragrance of time
Gone by, yet over in passing
it lasts
Like an unforgotten wine

This trip through mind is
part of the treasure
That fills my life to the brim
To share it with you just
completes the picture
The tree now has its trim

A LONG WAY TO GO

What do you tell your sons
of the days to come
When gloom hangs bleak
in an age of dread
that gnaws with
groans and fears.

Crime is old
that was just a start.
seize and hold
maim, wipe out
the cold game of hate
that's for us

The scene is not
right from wrong,
or good from bad
it's grey all grey
by whose rule is my want
your need

I tell you this
They will need God's help
They can not drift on the
others gain
like we
whose 'needs' now pass
the dreams of youth.

Did I learn to curb my wants?
Did I earn the right to teach?
No, they must learn from God,
within.
If I can but point the way,
my work is done.

But will they hear?
Will they see
the need to try?
How bad must it get
for God
to make his move?

January 1980

TO LISA AND LARA

Our dearly loved daughters,

Sweet nectar in the morning,
fresh dew in the sunshine
two drops
sparking in a rose petal are
you two
dancing in the sight of God.

The joy of your passion
excites the breast
of the dove
In the early dawn,
at the softness of your love,
the butterflies blush.

With glistening eyes
and pounding heart
we see you two together.
our God we know
will keep you close
fear is gone forever.

God sees your love,
he hears your cry,
He listens to your hearts'
desire
rejoicing
that He made mankind,
now with hearts on fire.

July 1989
Indonesia, Jakarta

GREAT GRANDMOTHER

Her favorite spot was
by the corn field.
Grampa would set her rocker
right beside the first row
where she could listen
to the leaves
and smell
the ripening ears.
She was blind now
but no matter,
her peace was
undisturbed
by the darkening clouds.

Collie at her side,
a handful of flowering weeds
strewn on her long white
apron,
the frilly lace collar of her
smock
as white as the
thin strands of hair
blowing over
that old weathered face.
Yet in spite of the obvious
years of toil
and memories
sad and old,
a quiet joy
cries out
to all who view her.

So here’s a toast
    to yesterday’s laughs,
    to to-day’s questions, and
    to the smiles of to-morrow.

Taken in 2001, Norway Bay, Quebec, sitting in front of Mark and Ann Baron's cottage.

FRIENDSHIP

TO MARK, A SPECIAL FRIEND

From time to time in life
    a special friend is found
    who adds a certain colour
    full of mellow sound.

As time goes by the colour warms
    and glows with kindled love,
    reflecting all the joys and tears
    born of Spirit from above.

To speak of joys and tears alone
    would picture incomplete
    the sharing of our growth in Christ,
    our strength wherein we meet.

Feel our love, o' special friend
    and know from whence we come.
    God has given you to us
    in Him, we are one.

Dec 4 1981

ODE TO DEAR DEPARTED FRIENDS

So sorry to hear you've made it big,
    and found the Horn O'Plenty
We had such good times right up to the last,
    not thinking of you as such gentry.
(Sigh) It's hard to compare a drink in the tree fort with a back seat portable bar,
But I guess the old image will have to make way for the fur-enshrouded star!

So on to a new circle of friends to enjoy
    the old ones were starting to bore.
And of course the idea of work for a living
    is a thought one must abhor.
All kidding aside, good luck on your
    venture,
I hope you find things to amuse.
And when friends ask, I'll simply explain
    "They made him an offer he couldn't refuse."

THE FORGOTTEN WINE

An ode to the Oslands, our
 fine host & hostess,
(With egg on our faces for
 not bringing this with us),
With thanks for the lovely
 evening we had;
In leaving good friends
 we feel terribly sad.
The food was delicious,
 the "gab" rather foolish,
With all of their "sex-thoughts"
 the guests were unrulish.
In the States we will
 miss those great get-togethers,
(With strange conversations
 of chickens & feathers)
But hope you will manage
 an occasional visit
Old friends in new places
 are really most pleasant!
The evening depleted your
 great wine stock, I fear –
So start re-stocking with this
 one – We return in two years!!

Bev and Joan

THE REMEMBERED WINE

A toast to the Harrisons, our forgetful
friends of good conscience
it's great to have you back.
'Tis easy to see how the sadness of leaving
is but part of the joy of return.
How sensitive the scene that draws
us together.
And what remarkable vibrations
in the face of caution.
Whatever we will be yesterday so were
we to-morrow
in the shadow of the moon our
memories will flow from time, to time
So here's a toast
to yesterday's laughs,
to to-day's questions, and
to the smiles of to-morrow.

Lyle & Adalene

CHRISTMAS BLESSINGS

Thoughts of peace,
Words of joy,
A heartful of miracles,
May you share to-day.

Happy Christmas

Dec 1977

LOVE AND PEACE

Winter sunshine brightening
the cold north wind
Smiles of loved ones
in a sentimental dream
Laughter of youth
amid the peace
These gifts of God
we wish for you
May your Christmas season
be filled with love and peace.

Dec 1979

QUESTIONING

O friend by the fire
why do you sit
and contemplate

Are you any less real
than I
Is that fire in your eyes
or reflection of my own desire

You never move, you
never change
But how different do I see thee
If I sit and
smoke your pot
Will you to my soul
fill any goal
Or will there be
An end of sight

Sept / 73

This dream of life depends upon
    my mind

In quiet meditation I focus on
    my mind.

My mind to you, to me, my God.

MY MIND

SEARCHING THE PEARL

The pearl of my thought
has no words, for there are none
The gap is all around to
    form a void
Which is an illusion. The pearl
is on a difficult plane
existing not by thought or word
but as experience
not of the intellect,
of the 'soul'
With effort, it disappears,
only to return in the
vacancy of mind.
How can I empty its
'thought-riddled nature'?
Where is the obvious absurdity?
    Searching the pearl?

AND THE TWO BECAME ONE

There is a tree
it stands alone
where others have been.
Receiving God's beauty,
standing in the tempest
always growing
The sinewey bark toughens with
each year's tender new branches
reaching for the heavens
When the storms break
every leaf glistens
with pride
And the sap runs pure from
the very trunk where the lone tree
came from two.

Sept / 73

EYES TO SEE

Here we lay a grain of sand
on the endless beach of human destiny
E'en as the tide
Our restless goals
shift to and fro.

Time alludes the eye
to see the rock foundation of the soul
gradually erode
as the sea comes again
and again.

Oh but watch the sea and
you will see
not the riddle
but the key.

For 'tis not in the coming
nor in the going,
in the wearing, nor tearing
in the making, nor taking
'Tis in the eye to see
What will be.

Sept / 73

NOSTALGIA

We behold the wonderment
   of joy,
As two petals observe the beauty
   of a rose,
The chill of autumn casts a spell
   of nostalgia.

Turning chores of yesterday into
   a musical spell of non-sounds,
   dreams become reality,
   frowns turn to smiles,
   hearts grow warm.

What is this magic,
   where has it been?
Will it keep yesterday
   from to-morrow?

Will the cries of to-morrow's children
   mellow again as warm shades
   of the turning leaves
And will our blood flow with joy again
As a mountain stream in
   a new-found path.

Oct 1 / 73

RAMBLING THOUGHTS

As bubbles in the falling brook, so the thoughts
run in my mind
From love to hate, hope to despair, from
God to the devil
The verse goes on, without rhyme or reason.

Last year's hair has grown long;
Eyes have turned into the depths, while
This year's smile has come to the surface.

The success of yesteryear is to-day's failure
And the applause dims into a rumbling roar.
Mr. Executive, where are the trees?
Mr. Worker, where did you go?

1974

JOY

An old couple touching,
that incredible sense of balance
as I walk down the street.

The ebullient power of will
rising from its sacred source,

The universal sound of spirit,
all manifestations of promised joy.

Feb / 80

MY MIND

Where are the farthest reaches of
my mind?
Material bounds and ties are not of
my mind.
Being here and now is only through
my mind.
This dream of life depends upon
my mind.
My strength, my bliss is directed by
my mind.
Soaring the skies like a bird, is
my mind.
In quiet meditation I focus on
my mind.
From birth to death my love is of
my mind.
Lives beyond and lives before all coming
from my mind.
Life, beauty, strength and power, a servant
of my mind.
My mind to you, to me,
my God.

HOPE

Ray of sunshine, flower of hope
Disappearing in the whispering firs
Where come'st your gentle magic?
O'er mountains, and seas
o'er clouds of doubt,
through the transparent leaf
    of life
and the briny depths
    on the glistening crown
        of golden hair
Bringing life to earth, or
    death upon the sands

WORM

Ah, how I've longed
for the coming of Spring!
the turning of sod
and warm rays of sun,
feelings of joy
and thoughts of fun.
I've grown
so slender and long
I can stretch and bend
and back again
shrinking and squirming
in the rain.
It's so good to be alive!

Then suddenly, plucked
from my freedom
and dropped
in a box,
in a mass of wormanity
struggling for nothing.
There's got to be better for me,
I'll get to the top
where there's room to move,
a chance to grow,
some air to breathe.
I don't belong down there.

Aaah!
What beast has rent my severed
half
lying 1ifeless,
now skewering my guts
and throwing me
to this watery grave.
What's happening?
If this is life
I'm glad it's done.

What's that chewing
at my ruptured end?

WAITING FOR YOUTH TO PASS

How can little children's world
expand between here
and the corner lamp post ...
trees of link fences
chaining my youth
to nothingness?

"Children must be children,
seen, not heard"
(non-addicted victims
of peddled education).
My parents are teachers but
will they ever learn?

Daddy's got a posting,
West Germany, with good behaviour
trips to Paris, England, Italy, Spain,
quite 1iked it so I'm told.
More education, in French, German,
military confinement.
Home I came with nothing
to show but costumed dolls
collected far and wide
and me? so what if I'm fat
who cares about me
providing I follow the rules?

Then into solitude, a guitar
my only friend.
Where am I going
what am I doing
do I feel better
thin?

SEEKING UNDERSTANDING

Don't talk to me
of God
I watched His cancer
eat the flesh
from grandfather's
bones.

I watched my sister wince
at the terrible knowledge
of ignorance.
Why can't she see the answers?
How can she stand
the pain?

Yet, there must be more.
These two I loved best
though their minds be simple
showed me a beauty and peace,
was that God
in their eyes?

So here I am
in all my imperfection
a woman without degree
full of feelings
unexpressed hopes and seeking
something real.

AN ILLUSION

How long we have worked and toiled?
How many beautiful thoughts were soiled
All for the sake of what?
The secrets they gave us as keys to success,
The system of merit and fair observation
Are a basket of shit!

We gave it a go and tried not to think
In the face of a problem we'd give it a
wink,
So all would be fine.
But after a while you have to consider
The nearness of life and how remote
We soon would be.

The guidelines we had were but ego-
seekers
But they worked so well as body keepers
They're hard to forget.
So if in a moment of weakness of mine,
I opt to go back to a way of the past,
Be patient my love.

The past has come to an end, I fear.
It just won't make sense for another year.

TO BE

When you try to break free of the rubbish,
Why do they laugh?
Why can't this life of ours
Cut the riff from the raff?

Do you have to be born a philosopher
To see the real?
Why should only
To me appeal?

I feel so full of life and love
And yet remorse,
So much was spent by accident
With no real force.

What have I left to simulate,
What life's undone
How can there by any mystery
If life's been won.

There cannot be peace, now or ever
For me or you.
Peace is death b'yond any doubt, for
To be is to do.

CONFUSION

God said,
  Why do you ask questions?
I replied,
  I must have the answers.
God said,
  What will you do with the answers?
I replied,
  I will put them in my mind and my
  mind will have peace.
God said,
  What will your mind do when it has
  peace?
I replied,
  I will marvel at the wonder and joy in
  the beauty of the earth.
God said,
  Is there any absolute wonder, joy or
  beauty?
I replied,
  I cannot see it because I am confused.
God said,
  You cannot see it without confusion.
I replied,
  Am I blind?

BUS RIDE

How close we sit
  yet far away,
  something in our common soul
  wants to touch.
But no. We lost the sense
  of single source,
gave up our original heritage
  and in its place
  put this foreign self.
So here we sit,
  saying anything unimportant,
  unrevealing.
  Well peace to you
    my fellow traveller,
    perhaps some day we'll meet
    and talk of God
    whose presence
    makes us one

Feb / 80

SEARCHING

What a pity the wars are gone.
The old and young find only song
To pre-occupy,
The presence of their mind.

They search, they find, an empty chest
Nothing will pound the heart in the breast
Oh for the cry of yesteryears
The quest is gone.

A bust they must,
pursue with lust
Else all is lost,
The hearts of frost

A man of sage
Should be a sage
But whose the fool
Without a rule?

A voice sounds out between the din,
But only a few close by
Distinguish the truth
And lack of sin
Now let's all join in

Who's living and who's not?
Yesterday's knight
We'll see again

For now just be content
To dream where e're you're bent
Another day, another place,
For all the human race.

Don't they see, the fools,
The game has no rules.
There is no competition
There's nothing to petition.

The room is round and so it goes,
Let's all pretend we have no toes.
For toes do not a picture make
The scene's the thing, all
for the take.

The song goes on
Anon, anon
Hello my sweet,
My love, my swan.

This is an example
of Lyle's writing
his thoughts on
whatever paper was
available.

CANADIAN
BIBLE SOCIET

BOOK STORE

BIBLES AND SUPPLIES FOR SUNDAY SCHOOL, CHURCH AND THE FAMILY - BOOKS FOR MINISTERS AND STUDENTS. GIFTS AND REWARDS

Phone 236-3910

315 Lisgar Street

Ottawa, Ontar
K2P OEI

Joy

Feb '80

That incredible sense of balance
as I walk down the street,
an old couple [illegible],
the ebullient [illegible] power of will
springing from its sacred source,
the universal sound of spirit,
~~in the realization of joy~~.
all manifestations of joy.
partially realized joy.

Bus Ride

How close we sit
yet far away
Something in our common soul
wants to touch
But no. We lost the sense
of single source,
Gave up our original heritage
And in its place we put
this foreign self.
So here we sit, conversing
about anything unimportant
making sure
not to reveal.

Well peace to you
my fellow traveller
Maybe some day we'll meet
and talk of God
whose presence
makes us one.

ACKNOWLEDGEMENTS

I am grateful for all of the support and encouragement I received in getting Lyle's thoughts into print. The following friends and family have kept me focused on my goal. Thank you to every one of you.

Jane Matthews, for your professional formatting and extensive time in typing all of Lyle's work. Your help has been invaluable.

To my daughter Lisa, I am thrilled that you decided to once again pick up your paint brush to create the beautiful front and back cover.

To my daughter-in-law Kiernan, for the time you spent planning with me and suggesting I include samples of Lyle's handwriting in the book.

Mike Abrokwah of Uncapped Publishing – you have been wonderful to work with.

I am eternally grateful to God for giving me the inner strength to not give up on this project. It is a dream come true to see Lyle's poetry in published form for the enjoyment of his family.

www.ingramcontent.com/pod-product-compliance
Lightning Source LLC
LaVergne TN
LVHW041126150826
845673LV00007B/2194
* 9 7 8 1 7 7 7 1 0 6 2 6 3 *